IS THE GAP THEORY CREDIBLE?

By
Dennis D. Helton

ISBN 978-1-7365344-1-0

All Scripture quotes are from the King James Bible

Address All Inquiries To:
THE OLD PATHS PUBLICATIONS, Inc.
142 Gold Flume Way
Cleveland, Georgia, U.S.A.

Web: www.theoldpathspublications.com
E-mail: TOP@theoldpathspublications.com

DEDICATION

This work is dedicated to my faithful wife, Christine, of 60 years.

Dennis D. Helton
February 2021

TABLE OF CONTENTS

IS THE GAP THEORY CREDIBLE?

Gap Theory Defined

Concerning biblical interpretations (exegesis) of Creation among Christians, there is a belief called "The Gap Theory." Actually, it is less than a theory because theories are based upon hypothetical circumstances which are merely assumed conditions. This gap theory is also known as "The Ruin and Restoration Theory."

At the outset, the writer states that he does not believe in the "so called" Gap Theory. However, many fine Christian brethren do believe in some form of it. Advocates of this theory believe that there is a gap of indeterminate (uncertain) time between the verses of Genesis 1:1 and Genesis 1:2. The claim is that a former civilization (probably satanic and possible human-kind) existed between the two verses of Genesis 1:1 and Genesis 1:2. This "alleged" pre-Adamite civilization was supposed to be guilty of corrupting earth. The gap theorists claim a gap of time, longer than a 24-hour solar day (?), occurred when chaos reigned upon earth after the first day of God's Creation. However, it would be hard to reconcile a proposed former creation of earth, with animals, vegetation, and human life, because there was no habitable earth (neither life forms) existing between Genesis 1:1 and Genesis 1:2. You would have to assume that an entire, finished world was completed at the end of Genesis 1:1. There is no mention of a formed world. Land did not appear until the third day of Creation (Genesis 1:9). Life forms did not appear until the third, fifth and sixth day. Conclusion: Neither an angel, life form, or a mortal man could exist upon an earth that did not yet exist.

Old Earth Gap Theorists

Some (not all) of the Gap Theorists are basically "Old Earth" and "Deep Time" advocates that seek to interpret the six days of Genesis chapter one as long days of ages rather than 24-hour days. We who do not believe in any aspect of the gap theory, are basically "New Earth" advocates of an earth-age of much less than 10,000 years (the writer believes about 6,000 years). Actually, the "Old Earth" theory lends credence to the wicked theory of evolution (or the anemic crutch of so-called "theistic evolution").

Disclaimer/Apology

There are many wonderful Christians who embrace the gap theory and the writer will not throw rocks at them...although he is in disagreement with their interpretation. These people may (?) have more light on the subject. The writer is sure that some of the past writers of the gap theory, as well as many present writers, may be much smarter than this country boy.

Origin & Contributors to The Gap Theory

The invention of the gap theory is credited to Dr. Thomas Chalmers (1814) along with George H. Pember (1876). Many writers have contributed to this theory in various teachings of Old Earth theories. Some of the contributors to the gap theory were genuine saved people and some probably were not saved, hence----C. I. Scofield, Clarence Larkin, Bernard Pallisy, James Hutton, Sir Charles Lyell, Charles Darwin, Dr. Steven Dill. Young Earth advocates (as this writer) tout the authored book by Weston Fields, "Unformed And Unfilled—A Critique Of The Gap Theory," as a commendable read.

Original Definition of the Word "Replenish"

One of the chief reasons for the belief of gap theorists is due to their speculation of the meaning of the word "replenish" (Hebrew "male") in Genesis 1:28. The gap theorists assume the word replenish means to "fill again, or refill." To them, this appears to imply that there had been a previous civilization that had existed; a so-called "pre-Adamite" creation. However, the Hebrew word "replenish" simply means "fill."

Again, there was no "completed" earth to fill between Genesis 1:1 and Genesis 1:2; there was only light and darkness (Psalms 74:16; 104:20). Even on the Second Day of Creation, there was only water above and below, without any dry land.

7

Consequently, a "refilling" or "filling again" does not fit an alleged corrupt earth picture. Land and herbal life did not appear until the third day. The writer believes that the true meaning of the word "replenish" of Genesis 1:28, is misunderstood by our "Gap Theorist" friends.

Again, it is not true that the word "replenish" means to "refill or fill again." Of course, in modern English, the word could easily be mis-interpreted and misunderstood to mean "fill again." However, the etymology [earliest literary meaning of the word] supports the simple meaning of "fill." In the OT, the Hebrew word "male" is translated only seven times as the Old English word "replenish," whereas it is translated "fill," "filled" or "full" some 250 times. The precise meaning is "fill." Of course, in the transition of time, English words have taken on different shades of meaning.

A Fantasy Civilization that Never Existed

Most gap theorists claim that there was a former pre-Adamite race of beings upon the earth between Genesis 1:1 and Genesis 1:2. In other words, many of the gap theorists believe that there were, in fact, two Creations, one interrupted by Satan between Genesis 1:1 and Genesis 1:2, and another later of Adam and Eve (that allegedly followed the satanic ruination of an alleged former Creation). This writer does not believe in a "Two Creation" theory.

It was an "unfinished" earth of no land mass and no life-forms between the two verses of Genesis 1:1 and Genesis 1:2. Again, the validity of a gap theory demands that there were two Creations: 1) a pre-Adamite race that corrupted earth (an earth not yet created or finalized) and, 2) the Bible ethnos race of Adam and Eve.

God said after each of the first five days of creation that it was good (Genesis 1:10,12,18,21,25). After the sixth day, He said it was very good (Genesis 1:31). If God's Creation had been interrupted at any time by some form of corruption, it would be highly unlikely that God would say His creation was good after each day of creation.

Two Kinds of Gap Theory Inhabitants

Some gap theorists appear to be divided as to whether or not this "alleged" pre-Adamite race consisted of satanic beings (fallen angels) or one of a corrupt human form.

As a young Bible student with meager Bible knowledge and an admirer of Clarence Larkin's writings and charts (who advocated a pre-Adamite race), the writer was mildly shocked and wondered about this imagined race of pre-Adamite beings of Larkin's claim (the writer still loves Clarence but disagrees with his theory of a pre-Adamite race). Again, our gap theory brethren claim that there was a great cataclysmic

9

event, probably caused by Satan, that occurred between the verses of Genesis 1:1 and Genesis 1:2, of the Creation. The pre-Adamite advocates assume a completed world at the end of Genesis 1:1.

Many gap theorist advocates believe that a human form of life existed between Genesis 1:1 and Genesis 1:2 because of their belief that the Hebrew word "was" of Genesis 1:2 means "became," which they assume supports the gap theory claim. Theirs was the belief that the previously finished world of Genesis 1:1 was victim of a turbulent, violent, polluted world by a rebellious civilization of either fallen men or fallen angels. The word "was" of Genesis 1:2 is defined by Strongs' Concordance, 01961, "hayah" (pronounced haw yaw), to exist, i. e. be or become, come to pass. Of course, our gap theorist brethren prefer become. Another definition of "was" appears in a combination word form of Hebrew "towb," (pronounced tobe), an adjective meaning "was good." So because of the different Hebrew words, hayah and towb, gap theorists base their belief on two creations, a world polluted by evil and destroyed and another world that was pronounced good by God (Genesis 1:25, 31). The Hebrew word "hayah" is also used in Genesis 3:1 where it is said that the serpent was more subtil, not became more subtil.

The same Hebrew "hayah is used in Exodus 3:14 where God says, "I AM THAT I AM." Now, God did not become, "I AM THAT I AM," He was always God at the beginning of creation and from the dateless past.

Angels Observed God's Creation

Does the writer believe in a pre-Adamite race? Yes, but it is not a corrupt human form or satanic race of entities proposed by our gap theory advocates. There was a creation of intelligent beings that were not involved in an "alleged" rebellion that supposedly resulted in a chaotic earth between the first two verses of Genesis chapter 1. We are told that the sons of God ("unfallen" angels) shouted for joy at God's creation (Job 38:6, 7). Obviously, these angels were created before the six days of creation when God created the earth, the stellar heavens, and mankind. These morning stars shouted for joy over God's miraculous power and wisdom, bringing glory to the Creator. God pronounced His Creation "good." This writer is not dogmatic, but it appears that the creation of angels (of the celestial world) may not have been part of the terrestrial creation of six days. Perhaps the angels were created in Heaven right before earth's creation.

Beloved Clarence Larkin

Brother Clarence Larkin (famous for his many Bible charts) erroneously assumed that there was a pre-Adamite race of beings (?) that corrupted earth and caused God to destroy it, even before mankind was created. Adam was the first man, or male "ad am" (I Corinthians 15:45) of humanity and Eve was the mother of all living, the first female "ad am" - (Genesis 3:20). Both Adam and Eve were called "ad am." If Adam and Eve were the "first" persons of human creation upon earth (and they were), there could not have been a former Creation of human-kind as some theorists claim. This erroneous interpretation would demand that Adam and Eve would only have been the first persons of a "second" creation. Neither does the writer believe that fallen angels interrupted or could even interrupt God's creation.

Critics of the Day-Age Interpretation

Gap theorists claim that there are problems with the Day-Age Interpretation. They claim that the Day-Age interpretation has death coming before sin (?), as in their own gap-theory; they also claim that the Day-Age interpretation contradicts nature in that, grass, herbs, and fruit trees were created on the third day before He created the sun to provide light for photosynthesis on the fourth day and insects to pollinate the fruit trees on the sixth day. Gap theorists say that it's rather difficult to see how this creation order would fit into a tenable Day-Age paradigm, in light of Numbers 23:19 (that God cannot lie). The writer believes we are talking about the supernatural Creation power of God in "origins" that transcends natural laws of the created. God does not confine Himself to natural laws of nature, of which He also created. Creation was NOT by natural laws of nature. Although God created natural laws for His Creation to operate upon, the Creation itself was of supernatural power.

The great error of the gap theory is that sin (chaos and corruption of a former civilization) entered humanity before the fall of Adam. The Bible expressly states that sin entered into the world by one man, Adam (Romans 5:12-14, 16-17). The entrance of sin into humanity, through Adam, is told in Genesis 3:14-19.

Replenish Definition in Noah Webster Dictionary of 1828

When the King James of 1611 was produced, the root meaning of the word "replenish" did not mean "to refill" or "fill again." The writer's authority on this matter is **Noah Webster's official 1828, "AMERICAN DICTIONARY OF THE ENGLISH LANGUAGE."** This dictionary is the English language closest to the King James Bible English. This authoritative "Webster's Dictionary of the English Language," says that the definition of replenish is:

1. To fill; to stock with numbers or abundance.
2. To finish; to complete.

This official Noah Webster Dictionary of 1828 certainly has more authority of the original meaning of the word "replenish" than modern dictionaries which reflect a modern shift of word meanings (sometimes significantly different from the original meaning).

Unlike the Noah Webster Dictionary of 1828, **the "modern" Webster New World College Dictionary (Copyright date of 2004)** gives a definition favorable to "refilling" or "to fill again" which reflects the modern change of word meaning. Noah Webster did not authorize the modern change of the word "replenish."

(**Note:** Noah Webster is universally recognized as America's greatest educated man. In 1807, Webster had mastered twelve languages. By 1813, he had learned twenty different languages; Chaldaic, Syriac, Arabic, Samaritan, Hebrew, Ethiopic, Persian, Irish (Hyberne, Celtiac), Amoric, Anglo-Saxon, German, Dutch, Swedish, Danish, Greek, Latin, Italian, Spanish, French, Russian, later adding Portuguese, Welsh, Gothic, and the early dialects of English and German. English, of course, was included in this list. So the writer favors Mr. Webster's original definition of replenish and believes it has much greater word-meaning clout.)

"Replenish" in Strong's Hebrew and Greek Concordance

Besides referring to the authoritative "**1828 Webster New World College Dictionary,**" the writer also decided to consult Strong's Concordance definition of the word "replenish." Following is Strong's complete definition: **Strong's H4390, "replenish:"** (Hebrew "male" - maw-lay;, maw -law'), a primitive root, to fill or (intransitively) be full of, in wide application (literally and figuratively):- accomplish, confirm, + consecrate, be at an end, be expired, be fenced, fill, fulfill, (be, become, X draw, give in, go) fully (-ly, -ly set, tale), [over-] flow, fulness, furnish, gather (selves, together), presume, replenish, satisfy, set, space, take a [hand-] full, + have wholly.

The writer did not observe a single instance of Strong's definition that supports the meaning of replenish to mean "to refill" or "fill again."

Having referred to "The Two Greatest authorities" on the definition of the English word "replenish," the writer is compelled to say, "Case closed."

Word Changes

Another classic, obvious change of word meaning that occurred over a period of time can be observed in the King James Bible and is well known to beginner Bible students. It is the word "prevent" of I Thessalonians 4:15. "Prevent" in ME (Middle English) originally meant to "precede" or "to come before." Prevent in Modern English has a different meaning than "precede" or "to come before." Of course, prevent in Modern English primarily means "to keep from happening."

Advocates of "theistic evolution" (not necessarily "gap theorists") also pick up on the "alleged" gap theory because they erroneously reason that it supports their theory that the days of Creation were not 24-hour days but days equal to millions of years.

What Advocates of a Demonic Pre-Adamite Race Say

Demons or Spirits of a Pre-Adamic Race? According to the Gap Theorist field of thought, a pre-Adamic race existed on an alleged, original earth even before it became "dark and void" (Genesis 1:2). These human-like creatures supposedly lived under the government of God and were presided over by Lucifer, the "anointed cherub that covereth" (Ezekiel 28:14). When these pre-Adamites joined Lucifer in revolt against God, a cataclysm fell upon Earth, physically destroying its inhabitants. Only the spirits of these beings survived to roam the earth, disembodied. This is offered as an explanation for why demons desire to possess humans, as they were meant to be "housed" in bodies of flesh and are uncomfortable otherwise.

There could not have been a pre-Adamite race of any sort living on earth during the 6-day Creation Week because....

1.) "...God saw that it was good." - Genesis 1:25. Actually, God called His Creation "good" seven times (Genesis 1:4, 10, 12, 18, 21, 25, 31). Neither was there a pronouncement of "bad" between Genesis 1:1 and Genesis 1:2.

2.) Since the earth (land) was created on day five and was pronounced by God as "good," no cataclysmic corruption led by Satan could have occurred during this time.

3.) If a cataclysm of a corrupt civilization occurred during God's Creation, which is spelled out in six 24-hour-days, two earth families would be demanded, yet the Scriptures are totally silent on this matter. There is not a hint of a "so called" pre-Adamite earth nor an earth of two Creations.

No Earth Existed Between Genesis 1:1 and Genesis 1:2

Again, there was no earth yet formed between Genesis 1:1 and Genesis1:2 unless you assume that a world was completed after its announcement in Genesis 1:1. There was no dry land (earth; firmament; space) which a race of beings could inhabit.

Also, the writer does not believe that God would allow Satan to interfere with His glorious Creation during its creation of six 24-hour days. However, following an unknown time "after" the completion of Creation, the serpent was successful in corrupting our first parents, the crown of God's creation, Adam and Eve. This led to the curse on the whole creation (man; beast; vegetable kingdom; earth) inherited by Adam's descendants (Romans 5:12).

Creation Days Were Solar Days of 24-Hours

Observe in the Genesis Creation Account (chapter one) that there is the term "evening and morning" stated after each of the six 24-hour solar days of Creation: the first day, evening and morning (Gen. 1:5), the second day, evening and morning (Gen. 1:8), the third day, evening and morning (Gen. 1:13), the fourth day, evening and morning (Gen. 1:19), the fifth day, evening and morning (Gen. 1:23, the sixth day, evening and morning (Gen. 1:31). The Hebrew word "yom" used for "day" means a solar day of 24-hours for each of the six creation days. A gap of time in the middle of a solar day of 24 hours (between Genesis 1:1 and Genesis 1:2) is incongruent (not in agreement; not in harmony with) with the Creation record.

(**Note:** Of course, the word "day" is also used figuratively and prophetically in reference to a longer period of time than a 24-hour solar day. We find this in prophecy and other indeterminate periods of time. In 2 Peter 3:8, one day with the Lord is **as** a thousand years and a thousand years **as** one day. In Daniel's prophecy of 9:24-27, a day is prophetically a One-Year duration and a week is a Seven-Year period. Daniel's 70th Week of Prophecy is the horrendous 7-Year Tribulation Period (time of Jacob's trouble – Jeremiah 30:7). The patriarch, Jacob, worked for his two wives (Leah and Rachael) for one week of seven years each, or fourteen years total.

Hebrew Words Denoted an Unfinished Earth, Not a Prior Human Pre-Adamite Civilization

Again, advocates of the gap theory also make the claim that the earth was in chaos, polluted and corrupted between the verses of Genesis 1:1 and Genesis 1:2. Genesis 1:2 says, "And the earth was without form, and void; and darkness was upon the face of the deep. And the Spirit of God moved upon the face of the waters."

Gap theorists claim that the words "without form" of Genesis 1:2 suggest some form of chaos. However, the Hebrew word "form" in Strong's # H- 8414, is "tohu" (to'-hoo), meaning desert, empty, without form, vacuity, nought. Obviously, this means an unfinished earth. Gap theorists also claim that the Hebrew word "void" of Genesis 1:2 supports a chaotic earth. Strong's # H-922 is

19

"bohu" (bo'-hoo), and simply means a vacuity, or unfinished earth. Gap theorists also use the word "darkness" of Genesis 1:2 to support their claim of satanic intervention. However, God Himself (not chaos), created the darkness when He separated it from the light (Genesis 1:3-5; Psalms 104:20). The writer does not see this to be the description of a chaotic intervention of Satan and his fallen angels (as most advocates of the gap theory posit). The Creation week was incomplete between the first two verses of Genesis chapter one. God pronounced his Six-Day Creation as "very good" (Genesis 1:31; 2:2, 3), so how could this be said of a created earth of an interrupted chaotic nature? The writer does not find the gap theory intervention to be a plausible (worthy of belief) theory.

Some gap theorists even dismiss the first two verses of Genesis chapter one, claiming they are not part of the creation week and that creation began later in Genesis 1:3; however, Genesis 1:1 states that earth and heaven began in Genesis 1:1. God could have created every part of creation in a moment of time if He so desired. but He did so as it pleased Him as outlined in Genesis chapter one. Of course, God's domain has existed from eternity past, but in Genesis 1:1, it is speaking of man's earth and heaven, not God's domain.

All of Creation Pronounced Good By God Himself

The gap theory advocates ignore Psalms 104:20 and Psalms 74:16 which say that God made darkness, day, night, light/sun and everything in six days (Exodus 20:11).

The "very good" of Genesis 1:31 "may" imply that Satan's fall (not his creation) be placed between Genesis 2:25 and 3:1. How could Satan cause chaos in a creation that was not yet fully created? Would God allow Satan to interrupt His Creation that did not even exist between the first two verses of Genesis chapter 1? The writer believes that the description of creation between Genesis 1:1 and Genesis 1:2 merely suggests that Creation had not yet been completed from its beginning. Why would there be an imagined chaotic period upon an unfinished earth (without form and unfinished) that was void and with darkness upon the deep? The earth was in its 'embryonic' state (unfinished). We can see an analogy of this of a human being. A person is conceived on the first day when the male sperm (seed) fertilizes the female ovum (egg). However, there are developmental stages up until the 9th month of natural birth. Even after birth, years are required for maturity. Of course, God miraculously created Adam in one day, fully mature; yet Adam resembled a grown man of perhaps 20 years of age...at only one day of age. Even Adam's creation was not completed until God breathed into his nostrils the breath of life. The miraculous Creation (earth; atmosphere; animals; vegetation; sidereal heavens (pertaining to the stars); etc., had the appearance of antiquity and long ages though only days old.

People of mere naturalistic leaning ignore the supernatural, miraculous workings of God and relegate most everything to naturalistic causes and effects alone. In vast contrast to the modern meaning of evolution, all beginnings and origins were of the miraculous creative works of God, not a "so-called" humanistic evolution of beginnings. Changes in various kinds or species do occur, but that is not evolution of origins.

Apology To My Gap Theory Brethren

The writer is not implying nor does he believe that genuine Creationists, who are advocates of the gap theory, believe in an evolutionary progressive creation (called Theistic Evolution). However, there are others that are weak (certainly not all) in the Scriptures and love to use the gap theory as an apologetic crutch to support their anemic theory of a progressive creation of long periods or deep ages of time. Periods of theistic evolution is congruent (agreeable) with modern false science of an earth age of millions or billions of years.

This writer believes the earth age to be

about 6,000 years. If there was a gap between the first two verses of the creation account in Genesis, the creation time would be greater that a 6-Day creation time.

Christians in need should cry out to God, "...Lord, I believe; help thou my unbelief" (Mark 9:23, 24).

Major Error Of The Gap Theory

Romans 5:12 says, "Wherefore as by one man (Adam) sin entered into the world, and death by sin, and so death passed upon all men, for that all have sinned."

This verse does not say that sin was in the world before Adam and Eve sinned. It did not say that sin entered the world because of the fall of Lucifer or the fallen angels. Old earth and gap theorists claim that sin (death and bloodshed) was upon the earth before Adam. If sin was upon the earth before Adam, Jesus had no reason to die for our sins. Again, we are expressly told that sin entered the world through Adam, not Lucifer.

The good news is that by one man's (God/Man Jesus) obedience, many shall be made righteous (Romans 5:19, 21).

Dennis D. Helton
200 Home Place Drive
Easley, SC 29640

ABOUT THE AUTHOR

The writer was born in Greenville, SC in 1934 and was a lifetime resident with the exception of two years in the US Army (Fort Jackson, S.C. and Fort Carson, Colorado) and two years residence in Florida.

After separation (honorably) from the US Army, the writer returned to Greenville, SC and married at age 27 to Christine Moore, an old acquaintance from an adjacent neighborhood. The Lord blessed us with six daughters, Debbie, Donna, Dale, Denise, Deree, and Dena.

A short time after marriage, the writer was convicted of his lost condition as a sinner and after a miserable time under conviction the writer confessed his sin and lost condition to God and was saved.

The writer was 40 years of age when he began attending college (3 years, no diploma).

The writer retired as a chemical technologist from Morton International Chemical Company in 1996. Before retirement, the writer had the urge to write on Bible subjects and wished that he had more time to study. Upon retirement, the writer bought a computer and became a novice writer.

The writer now resides in Easley, S.C.

D. Helton has written several documents as well as the book, "Jesus is God" available here: http://www.theoldpathspublications.com/Pages/Auth ors/Helton.htm#God

www.ingramcontent.com/pod-product-compliance
Lightning Source LLC
Chambersburg PA
CBHW051052030426
42339CB00006B/312